To

From

A Little Spoonful of
Chicken Soup for the Couple's Soul™

Published by Blessings Unlimited, Pentagon Towers
P.O. Box 398004, Edina, MN 55439

Design by Lecy Design

ISBN 1-58375-544-6
Printed in Mexico

Chicken Soup for the Couple's Soul™

Someone
to Watch
Over Me

$\mathcal{T}$he passengers on the bus watched sympathetically as the attractive young woman with the white cane made her way carefully up the steps. She paid the driver and, using her hands to feel the location of the seats, walked down the aisle and found the seat he'd told her was empty. Then she settled in, placed her briefcase on her lap and rested her cane against her leg.

It had been a year since Susan, thirty-four, became blind. Due to a medical misdiagnosis she had been rendered sightless, and she was suddenly thrown into a world of darkness, anger, frustration and self-pity. Once a fiercely independent woman, Susan now felt condemned by this terrible twist of fate to become a powerless, helpless burden on everyone around her. "How could this have happened to me?" she would plead, her heart knotted with anger. But no matter how much she cried or ranted or prayed, she knew the painful truth—her sight was never going to return.

A cloud of depression hung over Susan's once optimistic spirit. Just getting through each day was an exercise in frustration and exhaustion. And all she had to cling to was her husband Mark.

Mark was an Air Force officer and he loved Susan with all of his heart. When she first lost her sight, he watched her sink into despair and was determined to help his wife gain the strength and confidence she needed to become independent again. Mark's military background had trained him well to deal with sensitive situations, and yet he knew this was the most difficult battle he would ever face.

Finally, Susan felt ready to return to her job, but how would she get there? She used to take the bus, but was now too frightened to get around the city by herself. Mark volunteered to drive her to work each day, even though they worked at opposite ends of the city. At first, this comforted Susan and fulfilled Mark's need to protect his sightless wife who was so insecure about performing the slightest task. Soon, however, Mark realized that this arrangement wasn't working—it was hectic, and costly. Susan is going to have to start taking the bus again, he admitted to himself. But just the thought of mentioning it to her made him cringe. She was still so fragile, so angry.

How would she react?

Just as Mark predicted, Susan was horrified at the idea of taking the bus again. "I'm blind!" she responded bitterly. "How am I supposed to know where I'm going? I feel like you're abandoning me."

Mark's heart broke to hear these words, but he knew what had to be done. He promised Susan that each morning and evening he would ride the bus with her, for as long as it took, until she got the hang of it.

And that is exactly what happened. For two solid weeks, Mark, military uniform and all, accompanied Susan to and from work each day. He taught her how to rely on her other senses, specifically her hearing, to determine where she was and how to adapt to her new environment. He helped her befriend the bus drivers who could watch out for her, and save her a seat. He made her laugh, even on those not-so-good days when she would trip exiting the bus, or drop her briefcase full of papers on the aisle floor.

Each morning they made the journey together, and Mark would take a cab back to his office. Although this routine was even more costly and exhausting than the previous one, Mark knew it was only a matter of time before Susan would be able to ride the bus on her own. He believed in her, in the Susan he used to know before she'd lost her sight, who wasn't afraid of any challenge and who would never, ever quit.

Finally, Susan decided that she was ready to try the trip on her own. Monday morning arrived, and before she left, she threw her arms around Mark, her temporary bus riding companion, her husband, and her best friend. Her eyes filled with tears of gratitude for his loyalty, his patience, and his love. She said good-bye, and for the first time, they went their separate ways.

Monday, Tuesday, Wednesday, Thursday.... Each day on her own went perfectly, and Susan had never felt better. She was doing it! She was going to work all by herself.

On Friday morning, Susan took the bus to work as usual. As she was paying her fare to exit the bus, the driver said, "Boy, I sure envy you."

Susan wasn't sure if the driver was speaking to her or not. After all, who on earth would ever envy a blind woman who had struggled to find the courage to live for the past year? Curious, she asked the driver, "Why do you say that you envy me?"

The driver responded, "It must feel so good to be taken care of and protected like you are."

Susan had no idea what the driver was talking about, and again asked, "What do you mean?"

The driver answered, "You know, every morning for the past week, a fine looking gentleman in a military uniform has been standing across the corner watching you when you get off the bus. He makes sure you cross the street safely and he watches until you enter your office building. Then he blows you a kiss, gives you a little salute and walks away. You are one lucky lady."

Tears of happiness poured down Susan's cheeks. For although she couldn't physically see him, she had always felt Mark's presence. She was lucky, so lucky, for he had given her a gift more powerful than sight, a gift she didn't need to see to believe— the gift of love that can bring light where there had been darkness.

Sharon Wajda
Chicken Soup for the Couple's Soul

LOVE IS THE MOST POWERFUL, MAGICAL FORCE IN THE UNIVERSE, AND THERE IS NOWHERE IT DISPLAYS ITS BEAUTY AND WONDER MORE THAN IN THE INTIMATE RELATIONSHIP BETWEEN TWO PEOPLE.

Jack Canfield and Mark V. Hansen

Love
Unspoken

$\mathcal{J}$ust home from a four-day stay in the hospital, I insist that washing my hair is an immediate necessity. It really isn't. A warm and steamy bathroom seems to be the perfect place for me to hide from the fear twisting around my heart.

I have postponed the inevitable moment all the way through undressing, and I have postponed it through sinking into the warm soapy water. But I can postpone it no longer. So I allow my gaze to slowly and cautiously drift downward. To the empty space where my left breast used to be.

It is bruised...green and yellow and filled with black stitches covered with dried blood. It is such an indignity, so brutally ugly.

Quickly I concoct exotic mental plans to keep my husband, Jim, from ever again seeing me naked. Mutual passion has been such a strength in our marriage. But now, all of that seems over. How could I entice him with a lopsided and mutilated figure? I am only forty-three years old, and I am so deeply ashamed of my body for this betrayal. I lie back in the bath, waves of sadness washing over me.

The bathroom door swings open and Jim walks straight through my cloud of self-pity. Not saying a word, he leans over to slowly place his lips onto each of my eyelids. He knows this is my most favorite of our private "I love you" traditions. Still silent and without hesitation, he bends further down. I brace myself for the barely hidden revulsion.

Jim looks directly at my wound and gently kisses the prickly stitches. Once. Then twice. Three times. He stands up and smiles lovingly at me. Then he blows me a special airmail kiss, my second most favorite tradition, and softly closes the door behind him.

My warm, grateful tears roll down my cheeks and drop gently into the bathwater. The bruise on my chest is still there. But the one on my heart is gone.

Margie Parker
Chicken Soup for the Couple's Soul

THERE IS NO MIRACLE GREATER THAN LOVE. IT IS GOD'S MOST PRECIOUS GIFT TO US.

Jack Canfield and Mark V. Hansen

The
Mayonnaise
War

$\mathcal{B}$ack when I was a new Christian, I used to brag that the divorce rate among active Christians was only one out of a thousand marriages.

Sadly, that argument bit the dust long ago.

In fact, as a bookseller and book reviewer, I'm noticing more and more titles on marital problems among Christians. After all, the vow was "for better or for worse," and as I look back on my own marriage, I see how many pitfalls have come from mistaken expectations.

My wife thought she was marrying Ward Cleaver, and I assumed every new wife stepped out of a Good Housekeeping advertisement, a can of Pledge in one hand, the other busily stirring the stroganoff and a seal of approval on her forehead.

19

Surprise—we were both wrong. I made that discovery the first night I opened the fridge to fix a sandwich.

"Hey, Honey...where's the Best Foods Mayonnaise?"

Silence. And then, "Darling...I don't use Best Foods, I use Kraft Miracle Whip."

Silence again.

Over the next several days, we discovered she liked Crest, I brushed with whatever was on sale. I liked green olives, she hated them and would only eat black ones. When I, shivering, turned up the furnace and the electric blanket, she was right behind me turning them down. Remembering her childhood, she liked to take Sunday drives—to which I would respond, "Yes, but that was when gas was twenty-nine cents a gallon. Let's watch an old movie instead."

The worst discovery of all was that she was a morning person, popping out of bed like a piece of toast, while I awoke with pajamas nailed to the mattress. "If God meant man to see the sunrise," I explained, "he'd have scheduled it for much later in the day."

The night we realized we both liked Ivory soap, we celebrated.

I guess that we discovered no disagreement is so small it can't evolve into a major problem, and that two monologues do not equal dialogue. But most of all, we learned we no longer belonged to the separate universes we once did as singles. Our task was now to forge a new universe, one in which we would inhabit together.

After all these years, I'm still a night person, and my wife is still a morning glory. As for Ward Cleaver, she simply has to face it. I'm probably always going to be more like the Beav. And I've come to realize she's more likely to step out of the pages of the National Enquirer *than* Good Housekeeping.

But we love each other—and as a result, she's come to like grits for breakfast (or any other time), while I finally understand that the garbage does not take itself out.

We now have separate controls for the electric blanket. I put on a sweater when I'm cold. And in

*the refrigerator, side by side like a pair of contented
lovebirds, sits a jar each of Best Foods Mayonnaise
and Kraft Miracle Whip.*

Nick Harrison
Chicken Soup for the Couple's Soul

THERE IS NOTHING YOU CAN
DO, ACHIEVE, OR BUY THAT
WILL OUTSHINE THE PEACE,
JOY, AND HAPPINESS OF
BEING IN COMMUNION WITH THE
PARTNER YOU LOVE.

Drs. Evelyn and Paul Moschetta

Getting
Connected

$\mathcal{M}$y wife Lisa and I were struggling to put out the small weekly newspaper we had dedicated ourselves to producing in Guthrie, Oklahoma. I wrote and Lisa sold ads. Many nights we would work well past midnight as the rest of the town and our children slept.

On one such night, we crawled into bed only to crawl back out a few hours later. I ate my cereal, drank a large soda, then headed toward Oklahoma City and the printer. Lisa matched our five children to socks and sent the older three off to school with lunch bags in hand. I was so tired I had no business driving. Lisa was so tired she had no business doing anything.

"It's seventy degrees, and the sun is shining. Another beautiful day," the disc jockey said cheerily on the car radio. I ignored him.

What I couldn't ignore was the need created by the large soft drink. I realized I'd never make it to the city, so I pulled into the rest stop on the interstate just a few miles from our house.

In her exhausted state, meanwhile, Lisa was practicing an all-too-familiar art form: calling utility companies explaining why the payment was late and begging for one more day of hot water and air conditioning. She looked up the number and dialed the electric company.

As I stepped from the car at the rest stop, I heard the public pay phone ringing. I was the only person there, but I still looked all around.

"Somebody answer the phone," I shouted just like at home.

It had to be the wrongest of wrong numbers, I thought. Then I heard myself say, "Why not?" I walked to the phone and picked up the receiver.

"Hello?" I said.

Silence. Followed by a shriek.

"Thom! What on earth are you doing at the electric company?"

"Lisa? What on earth are you doing calling the pay phone at a rest stop?"

We went through "I can't believe this" all the way to "This is downright spooky." I expected Rod Serling to come walking past to the Twilight Zone theme.

We stayed on the phone, and our exclamations changed to conversation. An unhurried, real conver-

27

sation, without interruption, our first in a long time. We even talked about the electric bill. I told her to get some sleep, and she told me to wear my seat belt and lay off soda.

Still, I didn't want to hang up. We'd shared a wondrous experience. Even though the numbers of the electric company and the pay phone differed by only one digit, that I was there when Lisa called was so far beyond probability we could only suppose God knew we both needed, more that anything else that morning, each other's voices. He connected us.

That call was the beginning of a subtle change in our family. We both wondered how we had become so devoted to our work that we could leave our children with a stranger to put them to bed. How could I sit across the breakfast table and never say good morning?

Two years later, we were out of the business that had so dominated our lives, and I had a new job with the telephone company. Now tell me God doesn't have a sense of humor.

Thom Hunter
Chicken Soup for the Couple's Soul

NOTHING IN THIS WORLD IS MORE POWERFUL THAN LOVE. NOT MONEY, GREED, HATE, OR PASSION. WORDS CANNOT DESCRIBE IT. POETS AND WRITERS TRY. THEY CAN'T, BECAUSE IT IS DIFFERENT FOR EACH OF US.

Justin R. Haskin
Chicken Soup for the Couple's Soul

Shmily

$\mathcal{M}$y grandparents were married for over half a century, and played their own special game from the time they had met each other. The goal of their game was to write the word "shmily" in a surprise place for the other to find. They took turns leaving "shmily" around the house, and as soon as one of them discovered it, it was their turn to hide it once more.

They dragged "shmily" with their fingers through the sugar and flour containers to await whoever was preparing the next meal. They smeared it in the dew on the windows overlooking the patio where my grandma always fed us warm, homemade pudding with blue food coloring. "Shmily" was written in the steam left on the mirror after a hot shower, where it would reappear bath after bath. At one point, my

31

grandmother even unrolled an entire roll of toilet paper to leave "shmily" on the very last sheet.

There was no end to the places "shmily" would pop up. Little notes with "shmily" scribbled hurriedly were found on dashboards and car seats, or taped to steering wheels. The notes were stuffed inside shoes and left under pillows. "Shmily" was written in the dust upon the mantel and traced in the ashes of the fireplace. This mysterious word was as much a part of my grandparents' house as the furniture.

It took me a long time before I was able to fully appreciate my grandparents' game. Skepticism has kept me from believing in true love—one that is pure and enduring. However, I never doubted my grandparents' relationship. They had love down pat. It was more than their flirtatious little games; it was a way of life. Their relationship was based on a devotion and passionate affection which not everyone is lucky enough to experience.

Grandma and Grandpa held hands every chance they could. They stole kisses as they bumped into each other in their tiny kitchen. They finished each other's sentences and shared the daily crossword puzzle and word jumble. My grandma whispered to me about how cute my grandpa was, how handsome an old man he had grown to be. She claimed that she really knew "how to pick 'em." Before every meal they bowed heads and gave thanks, marveling at their blessings: a wonderful family, a good fortune, and each other.

But there was a dark cloud in my grandparents' life: my grandmother had breast cancer. The disease had first appeared ten years earlier. As always, Grandpa was with her every step of the way. He comforted her in their yellow room, painted that color so she could always be surrounded by sunshine, even when she was too sick to go outside.

Now the cancer was once again attacking her body. With the help of a cane and my grandfather's steady hand, they still went to church every morning. But my grandmother grew steadily weaker until, finally, she could not leave the house anymore. For a while, Grandpa would go to church alone, praying to God to watch over his wife. Then one day, what we all dreaded finally happened. Grandma was gone.

"Shmily." It was scrawled in yellow on the pink ribbons of my grandmother's funeral bouquet. As the crowd thinned and the last mourners turned to leave, my aunts, uncles, cousins and other family members came forward and gathered around Grandma one last time. Grandpa stepped up to my grandmother's casket and, taking a shaky breath, he began to sing to her. Through his tears and grief, the song came, a deep and throaty lullaby.

Shaking with my own sorrow, I will never forget that moment. For I knew then that, although I couldn't begin to fathom the depth of their love, I had been privileged to witness its unmatched beauty.

S-h-m-i-l-y: See How Much I Love You.

Thank you, Grandma and Grandpa, for letting me see.

Laura Jeanne Allen
Chicken Soup for the Couple's Soul

Forever
Young

$\mathcal{S}$omething very strange has happened over the course of my twenty-six-year marriage. My parents have grown older. Our children are ready to leave the nest. But I have not aged. I know the years have passed because I can feel the losses. Gone are the size-twelve jeans and platform shoes. Gone is the eager face of a young girl ready to meet any challenge. But somehow, like Tinkerbell, I have been suspended in time. Because in the eyes and soul of my husband...I am still, and will always be...eighteen, as carefree and whimsical as the day we met.

He still calls me his "cutie." He takes me to scary movies, where we sit in a theater filled with scream-ing teenagers. We hold hands and share popcorn, just as we did so many years ago. We still chase fire engines and eat at diners and listen to sixties rock and roll.

"You would look good in that" he says, pointing to a beautiful girl walking in the mall. She has blond hair flowing down the middle of her back and is wearing a tank top and short-shorts. Did I mention she's about twenty? I want to laugh out loud, but I know better. He's serious.

Every July, he takes me to the county fair. On a hot summer night, we stroll across dusty fairgrounds taking in the sights and sounds. We eat corn on the cob, and he buys me tacky souvenirs. Pitchmen call out to us from booths along the midway. He throws darts at a board of balloons, trying year after year to win the giant stuffed bear. While others our age are stopping to rest on benches, we're riding the rides. Up, down and around, we're holding on tight as the creaking wheels of the roller coaster make their final loop. As the evening hours come to an end, we're at our favorite place, high on top of the Ferris wheel, sharing pink cotton candy and looking out at a sea of colorful neon lights below.

Sometimes I wonder if he realizes that I have passed four decades. That the children I bore could have children of their own. Doesn't he notice the beginning gray hairs? The lines around my eyes? Does he sense my insecurities? Hear my knees crack when I bend? I watch him...watching me...with young playful eyes, and know that he does not.

In four more decades, I often wonder where we will be. I know we'll be together, but where? In a retirement home? Living with our children? Somehow, these images do not fit. Only one picture is constant and clear. I close my eyes and look far into the future...and I see us...an old man and his cutie. I have white hair. His face is wrinkled. We are not sitting in front of a building watching the world go by. Instead we are high atop a Ferris wheel, holding hands and sharing pink cotton candy under a July moon.

Shari Cohen
Chicken Soup for the Couple's Soul

THERE ARE MOMENTS WHEN LOVE CAN
BE EXPERIENCED AS QUITE ORDINARY,
EXPRESSED IN A SIMPLE SMILE OF
ACCEPTANCE FROM YOUR BELOVED.

Jack Canfield and Mark V. Hansen

A Legend
of Love

Edward Wellman bade good-bye to his family in the old country headed for a better life in America. Papa handed him the family's savings hidden in a leather satchel. "Times are desperate here," he said, hugging his son good-bye. "You are our hope." Edward boarded the Atlantic freighter offering free transport to young men willing to shovel coal in return for the month-long journey. If Edward struck gold in the Colorado Rockies, the rest of the family could eventually join him.

For months, Edward worked his claim tirelessly, and the small vein of gold provided a moderate but steady income. At the end of each day, as he walked through the door of his two-room cabin, he yearned for the woman he loved to greet him. Leaving Ingrid behind before he could officially court her had been his only regret in accepting this American adventure. Their families had been friends for years and for as long as he could remember, he had secretly hoped to make Ingrid his wife. Her long, flowing hair and radiant smile made her the most beautiful of the Henderson sisters. He had just begun sitting by her at church picnics and making up silly reasons to stop by her house, just so he could see her. As he went to sleep in his cabin each night, Edward longed to stroke her auburn hair and hold her in his arms. Finally, he wrote to Papa, asking him to help make this dream come true.

After nearly a year, a telegraph came with a plan to make his life complete. Mr. Henderson had agreed to send his daughter to Edward in America.

Because she was a hardworking young woman with a good mind for business, she would work alongside Edward for a year to help the mining business grow. By then both families could afford to come to America for their wedding.

Edward's heart soared with joy as he spent the next month trying to make the cabin into a home. He bought a cot for him to sleep on in the living area and tried to make his former bedroom suitable for a woman. Floral cloth from flour sacks replaced the burlap-bag curtains covering the grimy window. He arranged dried sage from the meadow into a tin-can vase on the nightstand.

As last, the day he had been waiting for his whole life arrived. With a bouquet of fresh-picked daisies in hand, he left for the train depot. Steam billowed and wheels screeched as the train crawled to a stop. Edward scanned every window looking for Ingrid's glowing hair and smile.

His heart beat with eager anticipation, then stopped with a sinking thud. Not Ingrid, but her older sister Marta, stepped down from the train. She stood shyly before him, her eyes cast down.

Edward only stared—dumbfounded. Then with shaking hands he offered Marta the bouquet. "Welcome," he whispered, his eyes burning. A smile etched across her plain face.

"I was pleased when Papa said you sent for me," Marta said, looking into his eyes briefly, before dropping her head again.

"I'll get your bags," Edward said with a fake smile. Together they headed for the buggy.

Mr. Henderson and Papa were right. Marta did have a great grasp of business. While Edward worked the mine, she worked the office. From her makeshift desk in one corner of the living area, she kept detailed records of all claim activity. Within six months, their assets doubled.

Her delicious meals and quiet smile graced the cabin with a wonderful woman's touch. But the wrong woman, Edward mourned as he collapsed onto his cot each night. Why did they send Marta? Would he ever see Ingrid again? Was his lifelong dream to have her as his wife forsaken?

For a year, Marta and Edward worked and played and laughed, but never loved. Once, Marta had kissed Edward on the cheek before retiring to her room. He only smiled awkwardly. From then on, she seemed content with their exhilarating hikes in the mountains and long talks on the porch after suppers.

One spring afternoon, torrential rains washed down the hillside, eroding the entrance to their mine. Furiously, Edward filled sand bags and stacked them in the water's path. Soaked and exhausted, his frantic efforts seemed futile. Suddenly there was Marta at his side holding the next burlap bag open. Edward shoveled sand inside, then with the strength of any man, Marta hurled it onto the pile and opened another bag. For hours they worked knee-deep in mud, until the rains diminished. Hand in hand, they walked back to the cabin. Over warm soup Edward sighed, "I never could have saved the mine without you. Thank you, Marta."

"You're welcome," she answered with her usual smile, then went quietly to her room.

A few days later, a telegraph came announcing the arrival of the Henderson and Wellman families next week. As much as he tried to stifle it, the thought of seeing Ingrid again started Edward's heart beating in the old familiar way.

Together, he and Marta went to the train station. They watched as their families exited the train at the far end of the platform. When Ingrid appeared, Marta turned to Edward. "Go to her," she said.

Astonished, Edward stammered, "What do you mean?"

"Edward, I have always known I was not the Henderson girl you intended to send for. I had watched you flirt with Ingrid at the church picnics." She nodded toward her sister descending the train steps. "I know it is she, not me, you desire for your wife."

"But..."

Marta placed her fingers over his lips. "Shhh," she hushed him. "I do love you, Edward. I always have. And because of that, all I really want is your happiness. Go to her."

He took her hand from his face and held it. As she gazed up at him, he saw for the first time how very beautiful she was. He recalled their walks in the meadows, their quiet evenings before the fire, her *working beside him with the sandbags. It was then he realized what he had known for months.*

"No, Marta. It is you I want." Sweeping her into his arms, he kissed her with all the love bursting inside him. Their families gathered around them chorusing, "We are here for the wedding!"

LeAnn Thieman
Chicken Soup for the Couple's Soul

INTIMATE RELATIONSHIPS TEACH US WHEN TO HOLD ON MORE TIGHTLY, AND WHEN TO LET GO.

Jack Canfield and Mark V. Hansen

Where
Love Lands

$\mathcal{N}$o one knows where love's wings will land. At times, it turns up in the most unusual spots. There was nothing more surprising than when it descended upon a rehabilitation hospital in a Los Angeles suburb—a hospital where most of the patients can no longer move of their own accord.

When the staff heard the news, some of the nurses began to cry. The administrator was in shock, but from then on, Harry MacNarama would bless it as one of the greatest days in his entire life.

Now the trouble was, how were they going to make the wedding dress? He knew his staff would find a way, and when one of his nurses volunteered, Harry was relieved. He wanted this to be the finest day in the lives of two of his patients—Juana and Michael.

Michael, strapped in his wheelchair and breathing through his ventilator, appeared at Harry's office door one morning.

"Harry, I want to get married," Michael announced.

"Married?" Harry's mouth dropped open. How serious was this? "To who?" Harry asked.

"To Juana," Michael said. "We're in love."

Love. Love had found its way through the hospital doors, over two bodies that refused to work for their owners and penetrated their hearts—despite the fact that the two patients were unable to feed or clothe themselves, required ventilators just to breathe and could never walk again. Michael had spinal muscular atrophy; Juana had multiple sclerosis.

Just how serious this marriage idea was, became quite apparent when Michael pulled out the engagement ring and beamed as he hadn't done in years. In fact, the staff had never seen a kinder, sweeter Michael, who had been one of the angriest men Harry's employees had ever worked with.

The reason for Michael's anger was understandable. For twenty-five years, he had lived his life at a medical center where his mother had placed him at age nine and visited him several times a week until she died. He was always a raspy sort of guy, who cussed out his nurses routinely, but at least he felt he had family at the hospital. The patients were his friends.

He also was very close with seventy-year-old Betty Vogle, a volunteer who wound her way into Michael's heart—not such an easy task—by doing his laundry and being there for him whenever she could.

There even had been a girl once who went about in a squeaky wheelchair who he was sure had eyed him. But she hadn't stayed long at the center. And after spending more than half his life there, now Michael wasn't going to get to stay either.

The center was closing, and Michael was shipped to live at the rehabilitation hospital, far from his friends and worse, far from Betty.

That's when Michael turned into a recluse. He wouldn't come out from his room. He left it dark.

His sister, a red-headed woman who sparkled with life, grew increasingly concerned. So did Betty, who drove more than two hours to see him. But Michael's spirits sagged so low, no one could reach him.

And then, one day, he was lying in bed when he heard a familiar creaking sound coming down the hall. It sounded like that same, ancient, squeaking wheelchair that girl, Juana, had used at the center where he used to live.

The squeaking stopped at his door, and Juana peered in and asked him to come outdoors with her. He was intrigued and from the moment he met Juana again, it was as though she breathed life back into him.

He was staring at the clouds and blue skies again. He began to participate in the hospital's recreation programs. He spent hours talking with Juana. His room was sunny and light. And then he asked Juana, who'd been living in a wheelchair since age twenty-four, if she would marry him.

Juana had already had a tough life. She was pulled out of school before finishing the third grade, because she collapsed and fell a lot. Her mother, thinking she was lazy, slapped her around. She lived in terror that her mother wouldn't want her any-more, so on the occasions when she was well enough, she cleaned house "like a little maid."

Before the age of twenty-four, like Michael, she had a tracheotomy just to breathe and that was when she was officially diagnosed with multiple sclerosis. By the time she was thirty, she had moved into a hospital with round-the-clock care.

So when Michael asked her the big question, she didn't think she could handle the pain if he was teasing.

"He told me he loved me, and I was so scared," she said. "I thought he was playing a game with me. But he told me it was true. He told me he loved me."

On Valentine's Day, Juana wore a wedding dress made of white satin, dotted with pearl beads and cut loose enough to drape around a wheelchair and a ventilator. Juana was rolled to the front of the room, assisted by Harry, who proudly gave the bride away. Her face streamed with tears.

Michael wore a crisp white shirt, black jacket and a bow tie that fit neatly over his tracheotomy. He beamed with pleasure.

Nurses filled the doorways. Patients filled the room. An overflow of hospital employees spilled into the halls. Sobs echoed in every corner of the room. In the hospital's history, no two people—living their lives bound to wheelchairs—had ever married.

Janet Yamaguchi, the hospital's recreation leader, had planned everything. Employees had donated their own money to buy the red and white balloons, matching flowers, and an archway dotted with leaves. Janet had the hospital chef make a three-tiered, lemon-filled wedding cake. A marketing consultant hired a photographer.

Janet negotiated with family members. It was one of the most trying and satisfying times of her life to watch the couple get married.

She thought of everything.

The final touch—the kiss—could not be completed. Janet used a white satin rope to tie the couple's wheelchairs to symbolize the romantic moment.

After the ceremony, the minister slipped out trying to hold back her tears. "I've performed thousands of weddings, but this is the most wonderful one I've done so far," the minister said. "These people have passed the barriers and showed pure love."

That evening, Michael and Juana rolled into their own room for the first time together. The hospital staff showed up with a honeymoon dinner and gave them two glasses of sparkling cider for a private toast. Michael and Juana knew they had moved many people with their love, and they had been given the greatest gift of all. They had the gift of love. And it's never known where it will land.

Diana Chapman
Chicken Soup for the Couple's Soul

INTIMATE RELATIONSHIPS GIVE US
THE OPPORTUNITY TO DEVELOP
GREAT VIRTUES SUCH AS COURAGE,
PATIENCE, LOYALTY, AND TRUST.

Jack Canfield and Mark V. Hansen

ACROSS THE YEARS
I WILL WALK WITH YOU—
IN DEEP, GREEN FORESTS;
ON SHORES OF SAND:
AND WHEN OUR TIME
ON EARTH IS THROUGH
IN HEAVEN, TOO,
YOU WILL HAVE
MY HAND.

Robert Sexton